Poems in the Key of Life ... a Journey

Poems in the Key of Life...a Journey
Anne Marie Brooks

ISBN 978-1-84728-020-6

Front cover photo by Anne Marie
Front cover design by Cristy Milner
Back cover photo and design by Russ Kick

www.wisdom-and-wonder.com

www.annemariebrooks.com

ambrooks100@hotmail.com

Foreword

I began this book almost forty years ago. Almost all of these poems were written from 1968 to 1982 (starting when I was thirteen), and there is only one new poem. I have a wealth of books in me, and this is the first to be realized.

As much as life changes, it remains the same. When I read the words I wrote almost forty years ago, they still seem crushingly familiar and real. Many are still completely appropriate, like the first poem, "WAR," written during the Vietnam War. Unfortunately, we continue to be warring with someone almost all the time, which is why I updated the poem to include oil. And the ending poem, "LIFE," is still my anthem.

This is the beginning for me of what will be more poems, stories, and inspirational works to help you through life and let you know that you're not alone. I assure you that if my life can be what I want it to be, anyone's can. It is all in the power of your inner thoughts and the strength you have within.

May you enjoy this book and may it touch the feelings in you.

WAR

Blood
Dead innocence
Hurt unnecessary to
Those for whom there
Is no guilt.

Pain
To young couples
Fatherless children
Mournful widows
Lonely mothers.

Wounded
Physically hurt
Mutilated men and women
Emotionally wounded
A tragic sight apart from all humanity.

Do these things bring peace?
Peace of what?
Peace to the dead who will prematurely
Miss the joys and pains of a long life?

Peace?
To the widow who is now alone
Without
Her man at her side.

Peace?
To the children who cry for their daddies
In the night and ask, "When will he be home?"

Peace?
To the mother who has watched her son or daughter grow
With visions of them in her mind as a happy
Prosperous person with a happy future.

Peace?
To the man who can no longer provide for
His family because he is unable to work,
Unable to hold his child,
Unable to be a complete
Husband,
Unable to live.

Peace?
To the emotionally disturbed—disturbed by the
Horrors of war.
He is unable to face the world,
To live normally
And
Treat his family normally.

Is this peace?

How high a price must we pay for peace? Or oil?

And is it worth it?

Both sides of war suffer the same sorrows,
But
Will war ever cease to exist?

Man's self-destruction may be the only end in sight.

▲

Gone and Alone

I wish I were gone
To the still, calm, peaceful waters,
And the tall green grass.

Where worrying and hurt are gone
And people are scarce
Alone
I'm all alone
For miles
And
Miles

No matter which way I go
I know—
I am peacefully alone.

▲

Happiness Thrives Alone

The things I write are filled with gloom,
Desperation and despair.

Of course, I must say this is where I get my inspiration.

To write of beauty is to waste ink.
The feelings of joy and sights of nature
Are to be enjoyed,
Not copied or played or molded.

But sadness, ah it can bring to
Others the warmth of those who have
Died in the same ways.

Misery loves to be understood
Happiness can thrive alone.

▲

In My Head

In my hollow head
I wonder what is dead.
Is it me?
Could it be?
I've gone and I don't know it.

In my half-crazed head
It looks like all is black.
There are no colors on the wall
All that's left is a long dark hall.

In my head I don't know what is going on.
I'd like to go somewhere and farm.
Cultivate my brain
I'm sure it would all turn out the same.

In my head I wonder why
Wish I could end it and die.
There's no use, no purpose
No reason to surface
From a life that's lived as a lie.

▲

CONFUSED

What do you do when you
Love someone or something
And
Hate it all at the same time.

What do you do when you
Want someone or something
And
At the same time dread it.

You cry,
You pray,

And when things get worse
You wish you'd die

But then— Suddenly ____________
A glimmer of hope will appear
And I'm cheered
But not for long.

Then the cycle begins again and
I hope I'll make it
Till the sun shines through
Again.

▲

NOTHINGNESS

Life is a mere illusion
Nothing really exists
There is no love
No hope
No understanding
No concern
There is no hate
No despair
No apathy
No tactlessness

There is nothing to look forward to
NOTHING!
I live in a world of nothingness.

NOWHERE

Life is a slow process of death
Each second is a step closer
To eternal peace

Away,   Away
Far away

To the everlasting pastures
Of total unfeeling

To nowhere

The Unfinished Poem

I want to go away
Where I can be me
Go away to stay
Where I can be free

There's nothing I wouldn't do
To have some peace of mind
If only I knew
A place of that kind

HA

Music from the past
It brings back sad memories.
Yet they are reminders that
At one time my heart was lighter.

I had the strength to carry
Whatever burdens life was
Handing me.

I had hope.

I thought when I grew up and
Took charge of my destiny
-ha-
that life would change.
I would change.
I would be happy
HA!

▲

CRYING

Crying does no good
So I do not cry.
My problem can't be solved
So I do not try.
Still it hurts
Motionless, stagnating pain
Yet no real feeling.
Too much want to ever be filled
And no hope
No will to fight.

Death would seem much simpler
Even so
I don't have the strength
To let go.

Joke on Me

Get me a gun
Just for fun
I'll pull the trigger
Doesn't it figure
No bullets in the gun.

So Am I

I don't know what life will hold
I do not know what is in my soul
I want a smile like that of a clown
I want never to be so rich that
I
Can afford to live in a world without dreams
Reality is hard and so am I
So am I
So am I
So am I
So am I

NOSTALGIA

I can remember sitting in bus stations
Watching the people scurry around.

I can remember lying on a train station bench
Trying to sleep,
Trying to remember where I was.

Hoping I'd like wherever I was going.
It seems sad somehow that all that's over.
It hurt but it was a certainty.

I was always where I didn't want to be
Now
I don't want to be at all.

▲

No One Around

Life is nice,
The sun is bright
When life for you is going right
You'll smile, be happy and laugh all day
But you'd be saddened to see another hurt
In any way.

You're kind,
You stop,
You try to help
Somehow
You did it,
You've helped
Everything's all right now.

But now you're in trouble and down and blue
And there's no one around
To
Help you.

▲

LOVE?

Do I really believe in love?
Is it attainable for me? For anyone?
Why do I doubt love so?

Sex I trust – no commitment.
Love – all or nothing?
Both – is it possible?

What is more important—love if it exists?
Or
Freedom if it exists?
Can you have either?
Can you have both?

Confusion again is reigning queen in my heart and mind.

▲

A Stream

I've known so many people
In so many different ways
They all meant something to me
And now that they are gone
Some of me is missing too.

Now that I think of losing you
Another little piece is being thrown away
Life will get a little bluer for a while.

Someday I'll put all my losses together and learn what they mean
But
Right now I only know I'm going to miss you.

I hope you miss me too

If you don't it will all have meant
Nothing.

ELU$IVE

People meet, talk, trust, love
And drift apart
Life is a flow of people,
Reaching out but not daring to grasp and stay.

No one is different though he may claim to be
He or she will also drift as will the rest of us.
We're all like the sea, in a continual motion, confused
And
Unstable.
Only not all of us know this.
Those who don't are lucky.

▲

Look at That Over There, It's Pretty

The road is long and dirty
And I'm so tired and weary
I want to get home
No more to roam.

It's been a long time since I've sat and looked at
A flower
I was too busy building ivory towers.
I hope now it's not too late
And
That there's still time for me
To enjoy the things I never saw before.

▲

I Was Yours

Oh, When you were soft, tender, loving and gentle.
I was yours like a falling dove.
Oh, When your arms encompassed me
Like a blanket of warm sand and
I was the shell of your affection.

Oh, While we are young
Let us see ourselves as beautiful stones
Reflecting the path of joy in sharing a path.

Oh, Love let us live with our
Heads held high and our hearts
Grasping at the wonder of each other

Oh, Love let us love
But
Never multiply.

▲

PAIN

Pain is all I know how to live with
I am strangely uncomfortable with happiness,
I can only write when I feel hurt,
When I have been let down.
But inspiration slips away when things appear to be going well.

I can trust pain,
I know it as a friend.
I mistrust happiness,
It has always
Slipped out when I needed it most.
Pain my familiar friend kept me from dying,
Stone cold, it kept me and keeps me alive.

▲

HELP

H
 E
  L
   P

Get me out of this prison
That has tied my spirit
To eternal damnation and boredom.

I was empty before
Now I don't exist.
I am dying a slow painful death
That as I watch
I know I cannot stop.

H
 E
  L
   P

He Is Gone

The world is what you make it
HE IS GONE.

The faces around me are smiling
I AM ALONE.

The music lingers in my ears
I AM AFRAID.

The sun is shining in my eyes
I AM LEAVING.

The world is what you make it
GOOD-BYE.

ALWAYS

Don't leave me hanging
Let me know where I stand
Am I yours
Once a week
Once every two months
Once a year.

Please send a schedule
I will honor it with my love.
Just let me know where I stand
If I stand.

As I sit here—alone
My eyes well up
I feel so alone
I always feel alone
I guess I always will.

I wouldn't mind
If
I were trying to be
But
I, oh, I'm so lonely
I need love.

I feel so desperate
So alone
I need you and I don't want to
I need warm, tender, caring arms
Around me
No matter how much
I try to pretend I don't
I need love whether I want to or not
Especially now I feel so lonely
But as usual
All I have is my myself and
My verse.

▲

PEOPLE

Happy or sad
Good or bad
People
Nice and sweet
Easy to meet
Take your time
Act real fine
People are nice
Sugar and spice
We're all together
For always and never.

REALIZATION

In this world of compromise and promises
I have finally awakened
There is no love for me
Not the way I want it to be.

There is no happiness for me
I will always live in depression.

There is no friendship in this world for me
I don't belong anywhere
I'm out of time and place.

There is no hope for me
I know what I am
What I will always be

There is for me only myself
I'm all I have
I'm all I need.

▲

SLEEP

Sleep is my rescue
Yet
I love the nights
I come alive, my mind winds up
It works and produces an outpour of emotions.
During the light of day,
I drift through life,
I feel nothing
I refuse to think.

Music placates me
But
It doesn't move me
Except at night.

Nights, I come alive
My soul leaves this mundane world.
I am eighty women with ten lovers apiece.

I am powerful.

I am sexual.

In the morning they've all left me, I am alone
To face the world I hate.

▲

REVENGE

I care little if my standards are different for myself
And for others. I am me and I must live with the person
Within.

This person has tried by all that is real to live without
Causing pain.
Never have I been able to hurt people I
Have loved, at least not intentionally.

I have hurt and have often rejoiced in my vengeance toward those I
despise.
I accept that and I accept any pain inflicted upon me by those who
openly despise me.

But

I will not and cannot condone or accept pain by those who
Supposedly love me.

Small unintentional slights,
Of course,
But
Gut-wrenching, burning pain and betrayal will be met with anger,
Revenge and a hate
Which
Will not dissipate until there is an equal amount
Of pain visible to me in them.

24 Hours a Day

It always seems I'm on duty
I know it's not necessary, or is it?
I always feel I must understand
And take care of people's mental well-being.

But what about my own?
I can never relax.
Just be myself, a regular, ordinary
Person.
I'm always analyzing and considering.
I feel it's something I owe people
When in reality
I don't.
Is this what I can expect forever?
I certainly hope not!

▲

I Am Alone

I don't care anymore about anything
I have lost my hopes, my dreams, my goals, my fears.
I want for nothing yet I need love.
I care little if what I do offends or hurts,
My heart is hard yet my mind is clear.

I must be strong and not dependent.
What the future holds I do not know and
I do not care
I live each day as if it were my last.
I have only one regret
I learned too late that

I am alone.

Making the Grade

Trying to make the grade
Can be a drag.
I guess I just don't believe we should have to grow
In a world as absurd as this.

What is the reason for logic and responsibility?
Why must I have so much of it?
I want to chuck it all
Nothing really matters
Except what you make important
And at this point nothing is.

People all trying to be things they know they aren't
Why can't the play stop?
Would it be so sad?
Would it be so bad?
To be what we really are.

People walking and talking as if they know where they're going.
They are fooling themselves.
What the hell is for sure in this world?

Not even death for they may find a cure for it yet!

▲

SMILING

Wearing a happy face is too important to people.
People expect you to smile and be cheery all the time.
Life may not always be terrible
But
That does not mean
It is always good either.

Smiling is something that should be
Spontaneous
Or
It is a lie.

A plain face does not mean anger or sadness.
It only shows reality.
People are not always happy.
People sometimes just are.

- **Next time you don't feel like smiling—don't.**
- **Let your face be itself.**

▲

SOMEWHERE

I should be somewhere,
Where I am not
I should be feeling something I cannot

In this world with much to do
I sit and do nothing
I want to see what life can be for me
Yet I see nothing

The buildings stand around me
Like an army of concrete soldiers
The people pass by me like
Leaves in a windstorm

I want to scream and shout
I am here
But who am I and
Where is here

The leaves would still rustle by me
The concrete soldiers would still stare
Unapprovingingly at me

And I would have lost my voice
And remain unknown.

▲

The days of summer are swiftly fading,
Fading into the night,
Like a dream I forgot to dream.

The sun shines brightly still
It radiates no warmth.
They are only bright rays that
Illuminate the darkness of my life.

Lost youth and faraway dreams
Seem ancient in my mind
Like an old tune that only
The melody remains and the words
Have gone.

It all seems so long ago and
Yet only yesterday
To smile innocently and carefree,
To laugh with abandon and
Enjoy with no thought for tomorrow.

Such are the joys of youth.

▲

RHYME$

What's the use
You're so cute
I can't leave ya
I need to feel ya
Put your arms around me.

Work for a living!
Is that life?

No hon
No fun
What a life
Without a wife.

▲

CHANCE$

All my yesterdays roll past me
Giving me both comfort and anguish.
Making me feel alive.
There is no pain without joy
Or
Contentment without agony.
Desire and passion are fueled
By
What is impossible
Only nothing can be impossible.
So everything else can be real.

Time travels and takes us on a journey.
The direction is within our control.
To be able to take a part of the past and couple it
With the future is the ultimate goal.

All of this and more is tumbling within my soul.
There is no confusion only an ache,
A peacefulness and
A yearning and
Frustration at the loss of a
Solution.

▲

The Friend

We ran through the rain together
Holding each other by the hand.

As we laughed at our wet selves
We wiped each other off with grateful care.

Our eyes smiled and told the tale of our lives.

We drifted into an understanding, unaware of what had begun
Until it was too late.

I miss what we had but it was never meant to last
We were both only looking for a friend.

▲

The Past

The past cannot be obliterated.
It's part of me.
It's what I am.
Some of it I miss.
Some of it I don't.
But good or bad,
It's me
And I'm NOT ashamed of it.
Not anymore.

I've made mistakes
But
That's life.
It makes me human
And
I'll be human again.

▲

U$ED

I feel like a Kleenex tissue
I am loved and needed till I am used.
Then I am discarded for a new one
I am useless until I am new for someone
And doing for someone.

Someone please love me for what I am.
Love my faults, love everything that is me.
Love me as I am and not for what I do.
I'm getting thin soon I'll be thrown away again.

▲

FEAR

I am afraid
Fear, old friend
You've come again
For another uninvited visit.

To warn me, I'm sure to be careful,
To take care of my heart.

I am afraid of love
I bear only scars of wounds
That time is trying to heal.
Why should now be different?
Love is just a word that is
Used so people can cause you
To bleed.
Deep red blood that never really stops flowing,
Until there's no more to give.

▲

FEELINGS

Feelings, some good
Some bad.
Feelings, I don’t want to know
Good or bad they cause me anguish.
To feel is to want.
And I don’t want to want.

▲

ANCHOR

You are my anchor
Yet you make my life
Rocky.

You are not one person
You are ever-changing
One day a blonde, the next day you're graying.

Sometimes you're nice.
Sometimes I hate you.

Too bad I can't live without you.

▲

The Magic of Music

It can take me back to happy times
To sad and lonely times, to people
And
Places, to dreams and hopes.

The nostalgia is soothing.
All the places I danced bring a smile
To my face.

When I'm there I'm in my own world.
Music in my ears, my body moving to the beat.
People smiling and feeling free to be who they are.
Sweat pouring off my body as the rhythm gets in my soul.

Bogart's, Ron's Haus, The Living Room, The Pump House
Multilevel dance floors, funky DJ's or bands
Disco balls, lighted squares on the dance floor,
Flashing strobe lights
People looking pretty

Those were and are the places that I can be me.
My soul is set free and I feel totally happy.
Not looking for love or even a person
To dance with.
Don't need one.
Feeling free enough to dance alone,
In my own wonderful world of music.

I am alive.

▲

Not Yet

I am not yet empty. There is still so much to say.
Rain on my skin dripping, as I'm soaked to the bone
Arms around me keeping me warm
A feeling of safety for a short time.

Such an ache when it has ended
Like a
Crater that can never be filled.
Do not trespass and off-limits are posted as this crater takes on a
Life of its own.
New emotions, not safety—definitely not safety.
Excitement, sharp ups and disastrous downs, schoolgirl's giggles
And womanly desires. The beginning of a new horizon and gratitude
For the ability to trust and to be shown the pleasures of desire.

Pain deep and lasting, a pain, which knows no limits. Pain for his
Pain
And
The knowledge that the only solution is to walk away.
To make it less difficult, to do the right thing, withdraw
When what you want most is to draw nearer.

A new and frightfully physical pain that has never eased.
Only when one is everything can you leave it and
Still possess it. Though the distance is great there could be
No sweeter or more connected a relationship
Than this, which was born out the deepest desires
And
Innermost needs.

It has grown and is an entity in itself
Which gives life and power and endurance
To our mated souls
No stronger tie could exist between a man and a woman,
No deeper a love.

▲

Thank You

Even though you are not here
You have helped
You send your help in your warm dreams
I feel I know you well and I tell
Myself the things I believe you would
Tell me.

I know if I need you, you are there
As you know I would be there
For you.

With you my heart feels no fear, no threat.
I know you have cared more for my fragile heart
And my sanity
Than you have for your own
Emotional wants and needs.

My trust and body I have given you
Freely
But
You have never taken advantage though many
Times you could have.

You make my spirit free and my heart light, you've taught
Me it's possible to fly and to laugh

Thank you for being my friend and love.

▲

SHARED

Words of past pain and misery
Make the present bearable.

In my verse, I always see such words
As death, pain, ache, hurt, alone, confusion and
Emptiness.
Feelings I live with still.
But the cause is different.

I share my feelings of "endless emptiness" with one soul.
A mate in feeling and understanding.

If two souls can share pain,
We do.
It makes your pain ache in my heart
And
My pain aches in your heart.
It is good to not be alone.

▲

PASSION

Ah, what a wonderful word
And better yet what a wonderful feeling.
Whether it is now in the present
Or a
Distant memory.

It makes your blood boil,
Your heart race,
Your thoughts
Are constantly of him

His touch, his voice
The smile on his face

Ah, how wonderful to know
That you elicit a passion
In him.

That he can't get you out of his head
That his heart pounds
And he sees you in everything.

Together, even better.
Passionate looks
Kisses
Bodies wrapped in each other
Feeling as one.

Too bad it lasts
Only as a memory
But one that can be
Fortunately
Found many times
In one's life.

The faces may be different
Or they may not
But
Ah, that wonderful feeling
Will always remain.

Golden Field

A golden field of bright sunshine
Only the sounds of birds
I lie there
Drinking up the peacefulness

Blocking all thoughts of civilization
For civilization is so uncivilized.

Thinking only of the sounds of
The birds and warmth
Of the sun and the cool breeze.

MEMORIES

When happiness comes and goes
I won't be bitter
I won't be sad
I'll just thank god for the memories I'll have

I know someday, somewhere, someway
I'll have a life that's full and bright.

It will not last but at least I will have a past
Not good, not bad but there
Just there.

▲

Never Apart

The sun brings a smile
In almost every situation
You succeed where even the sun
Falls short.
I sit on the apex
And
I lie in the valley
Yet your hand guides me through,
My thirst for you is unquenchable
Your well deep enough to keep
Me
Drinking forever
I am a blanket of flannel and satin
To warm and thrill you
For
We will never be apart in the heart.

▲

DARKNESS

Darkness descends on the city
Like a worn-out tattered blanket
Friends and family are really
Apathetic strangers and only the bums smile.

Everyone is in a hurry to go nowhere,
Everyone rushes to accomplish nothing,
Everyone gets upset over the trivial.
Stop and reflect.

All one can do is the best they see fit.
The world will not end if we mess up,
We are not that significant.
Those who love us won't stop.
Do not intentionally or thoughtlessly
Hurt another and you can at least
Be proud of your life.
No matter how mundane and dark it may seem.
For you will own your own soul
That is rare in this world of today.

▲

TOGETHER

When we are dead
I know we will be together.
Our lives have not been what
We would have had them be.

Full of pain, mistakes and emptiness
And poor timing.

We will be together in death, no longer
Lonely, no longer pained
As our souls touched in life so will they in death.

We will touch and be happy.

▲

Wisps of Love

A drive down a familiar road with music from the past
Paving the way. Warm and spring-like weather,
The sun shining and breeze crisp.
Familiar smells and texture of a warm hand on mine.
Your voice ringing softly in my ears as I turn to answer.
I realize you're not there. It's just my imagination
Very strong wish fulfillment fantasy bringing it all back.

The excitement, the feeling of wanting to jump up
And tell everyone how I feel and that my excitement
Is a physical experience that tingles from head to toe.

But silence is all there is.
Turning and my essence leaves me
And
Entwines in every way with the essence of you.

We are enmeshed in every way
But
The physical.
Two kindred spirits who feel together.

Such intensity is rarely found and is almost
Always nurtured by adversity and separateness.

And this we have in abundance.
The future is unknown and as such
It holds an array of possibilities which
Includes our joining the spirit and the flesh in
An embrace that will melt us into a state of rapture
And ecstasy and take us to a higher level.

It is not merely sexual, it goes beyond and is a total
Experience.
Body and spirit and self.

Giving freely and without
Inhibition of our souls, ourselves.

Letting go of fears and thoughts that chain
Us to reality.

We would soar like eagles and feel free and safe and warm.
Lying in the afterglow of our journey,
Still
Reality
Kept at bay as we linger in each other's arms,
Alone,
The only two people in the world.

No concerns, no worries just each other,
Soothing and caring for all old wounds and hurts until
They exist no longer.
This would never end even as we went our separate
Ways.

Until we came together again the strength and revitalization would nourish and keep us going.
The connection would remain intact and we would continue to experience
Each other's joys and sorrows.

What more could we want than that which we already
Have.

We have each other and this is everything.

▲

Transcended Love

It was a clear crisp dawn as she walked down the path that led to the pond. She loved the way the air smelled, so fresh and clean. She was feeling peaceful yet lonely. She went and sat by the pond, looking in to see her reflection smiling back. Suddenly, she was not alone. Next to her reflection in the pond was that of a man. He was smiling at her. The woman lay back in the grass and closed her eyes. His smiling face remained in her mind. She embraced the image with all her senses. She made it feel real, as real as when he had actually held her and stroked her. It was not her vivid imagination alone that brought him to her.

Hundreds of miles away, a man sits at his desk, looking into space. He is thinking intently of a woman that he's loved and who has loved him. A woman with whom he'd felt secure. He holds her close and she touches his face gently. They are sharing a love that seems to have transcended time and distance, that special feeling that continues to grow.

A warm breeze is her moist breath; sunny days are his intense eyes. Everything around them holds some little part of the other; with this they become more secure. She thinks of him and he thinks of her; with their memories meeting they feel the reality of each other and smile. They know they will never be alone.

▲

The Sun

I feel such unfamiliar feelings
I look at the sun
I see your face
But whether you care or not
Doesn’t seem to matter.

I look around at other people
Many are hurting because THEY
Care if YOU don’t

I love the sun and I won’t
Let anyone make me hurt
So bad that I can’t enjoy it

So many people become sick
Because they let their hearts
Be broken
My heart is wrapped in rubber
I always bounce back

Just so I can love the sun.

▲

The Act of Freedom

It is hard to live in two worlds
One where I am free and uninhibited
I can love who I want
How I want
Or
Not at all.

The other world is full of responsibility
And practicality
You must do this and do that
And do it whether you understand it or not.

Part of me won't let the other part be free
And one part is afraid not to be.

I hope with age and experience
I may combine the two
And be really free in me.

▲

Quiet noise, cool breeze
Comforting smog and
Broken wine bottles

Undernourished and broke
Home is a freight car
Gin for breakfast

Irresponsible and undependable
Sweet sleep
A thousand years from here.

White-pink cool breeze
Space when I need it
Concrete when I need it
Trees when I need it
Sand when I need it
Always alone.

White-pink cool breeze
Wake up to find
This is eternity
And
I have died.

Sweet cool soft breeze
Cradle me forever safe
Peace in my space, my concrete,
My trees, my sand, and my aloneness

No longer empty
No longer confused
Or tortured by reality

Just a cool soft white-pink breeze
Encompassing me forever
White-pink breeze.

▲

Without You

Broken-hearted, tired and weak
Looking for a place of solitude
To weep.

My world has shattered
I feel lost and battered
Alone in a big world
Alone with everyone
But without you.

Where Did I Go

I wonder what has happened
To the girl who once was me.
I wonder what she saw that
Changed her and made her leave me.

Was it the sight of everything that wasn't right?
Or
Was it that she knew it would never change?

She was such a hopeful person
She trusted me to take care of her
And show her how good life could be

Wasn't it enough that I gave her what potential she had?
Or
Did it scare her?

Will she ever return to me?
I so long to be the girl I used to be.

She needed love but I couldn't give it her and I couldn't find it for
Her.

I think it killed her
I think I killed her
My burial will be our rest.

▲

LIFE

Be alert,
Keep your eyes open.
Smile,
But not too brightly.
Laugh,
But not too loudly.
Love,
But not too deeply
Follow these rules, my friend.
Life will not be glorious
But
Your hurt
Will not linger.

▲

Afterword

I hope you have enjoyed this book of poems. I assure you it is not the last of my works that you'll have a chance to read. I would like to share a little more about myself, for after reading this you should know who I am.

I was born in Rhode Island and grew up primarily with my mother, who was loving but mentally ill. I left home at eighteen and worked my way through college, husbands, and relationships. I have a Bachelor's degree in psychology and a Master of Education degree. I'm currently working on a Ph.D. in parapsychic science.

I'm a veteran. I was a practicing therapist for over twenty-five years and have done everything from factory work to being the vice president of a behavioral health system. I've gone from Catholic to atheist to spiritual. I believe in myself and humanity and the universe as ways to find a better way to live and love and build a healthier planet.

I'm still on my journey, and with age come wisdom and wonder. I realize just how much I still don't know. I have so much to learn and to share. And I hope you'll follow me on this journey. I hope you enjoy your own journey every single step of the way. Even when things go wrong, believe in yourself and your dreams.

Peace
Love
Thank you

My Thanks

I want to thank all the people who have crossed my path so far. This book is about you and the impact you have had on my journey through life.

I want to give special thanks to my parents (deceased); my partner Russ for all his support and book-writing assistance (he's a well-known author—check out mindpollen.com for more on his works); my daughter and light of my life, Jennifer (I never felt anything but happiness with her, which is why there are no poems about her); my beautiful grandson Lucas; my friend Cristy for all her care and understanding and the beautiful front cover, which she graciously did for me; and Jeff, my shaman, who inspired me to publish this book.

Also, thanks to Jane and Russ, my brother Roland, Lisa, Darrell, Brett, Michele, Rena, Fred, Davena, Lisa B.W., Elizabeth, Christy, Ruthanne, Lando, my ex-husbands, and all my other wonderful friends and family.

And to all the wonderful poets who inspired me:
Peter McWilliams, Dorothy Parker, Langston Hughes, Rod McKuen,
Ezra Pound, Edna St. Vincent Millay,
and so many others.

www.ingramcontent.com/pod-product-compliance
Ingram Content Group UK Ltd.
Pitfield, Milton Keynes, MK11 3LW, UK
UKHW041920190726
13854UKWH00003B/1344